T0271709

THE DIVORCE JOURNAL FOR KIDS

First published in Great Britain in 2021
by Jessica Kingsley Publishers
An Hachette Company

1

Copyright © Sue Atkins 2021
Illustrations copyright © Amy Bradley 2021

A CIP catalogue record for this title is available from the
British Library and the Library of Congress

ISBN 978 1 78775 706 6
eISBN 978 1 78775 707 3

Printed and bound in Great Britain by Bell & Bain Limited

Jessica Kingsley Publishers' policy is to use papers that are
natural, renewable and recyclable products and made
from wood grown in sustainable forests. The logging and
manufacturing processes are expected to conform to the
environmental regulations of the country of origin.

Jessica Kingsley Publishers
Carmelite House
50 Victoria Embankment
London EC4Y 0DZ

www.jkp.com

With thanks to Tanya Gordon

THE
DIVORCE
JOURNAL
FOR KIDS

Sue Atkins

Illustrated by Amy Bradley

....
: :
: This journal belongs to :
: :
: _ _ _ _ _ _ _ _ _ _ _ _ _ _ _ _ _ _ :
: :
....

Jessica Kingsley Publishers
London and Philadelphia

HOW TO USE THIS JOURNAL: A NOTE FOR ADULTS

Separation and divorce are traumatic events for families. This journal is designed to help children express, explore and understand some of the strong emotions that they may be feeling and to help them process the divorce for themselves.

Encouraging children to keep a journal is a very simple, but powerful way to support them.

> "Oh, it's a storage box for your emotions."
>
> Xavier Sullivan, aged 10

As caring adults, we can help by simply acknowledging and listening to how a child may be feeling, without trying to "fix it". This journal is designed to support open and honest communication and to help children feel heard, understood and supported during a time of great upheaval. It is recommended that you read and work through the journal together.

Further suggestions for parents, teachers, counsellors and therapists on how to get the most out of this journal are included in the back of the book.

AN INTRODUCTION TO YOUR JOURNAL

"Divorce" is one of the scariest words that you can ever hear because it means there will be lots of changes and that can be upsetting and frightening. Things will be different and that can be worrying. But all through our lives we are all learning to handle changes. Just think back to when you were a baby and to where you are now – you've grown and gone from being a helpless baby to an independent toddler, to riding a bike and doing up your own shoelaces, to now doing lots of things for yourself.

When your parents tell you that they're getting divorced, there are many really strong feelings you might have – from anger, fear or sadness to feeling confused. Sometimes you feel all these emotions at the same time. It can all feel a bit overwhelming.

Divorce is sad and scary for everyone in the family and although you may know many kids whose parents are divorced, you might never have imagined it would happen to your family.

You might have lots of questions, thoughts, feelings and things you wish you could say or even scream very loudly at your parents! This Journal will help you express your feelings and get your jumbled thoughts out into the open so that you can make sense of them.

WHY KEEP A JOURNAL?

Nobody knows for sure quite why it works, but writing down your thoughts and feelings for just a few minutes every day, seems to really help people feel better.

It's really important to get your feelings out of your body as it helps you to feel more relaxed and calm. It also helps you to understand and make sense of what you are going through and helps you to sleep better.

Releasing your negative feelings in a healthy way by writing in your Journal is loads better than punching a school friend in the playground or shouting at your sister or suffering in silence.

It's healthy to let your feelings out. Otherwise it's like shaking a can of soda with the lid still on - the bubbles have got nowhere to go so they stay inside and when you do open the can it explodes all over you – and that's not a good idea! Your pent-up emotions will come out in the wrong place or may stay stuck inside you and that will give you a tummy ache or a headache and isn't good for you long term. So write, draw and doodle in your Journal – it will help you to feel better.

Trust your feelings – you are entitled to feel angry, sad, frightened, uncertain and upset while you go through all these changes to your family life. But things will settle down and get easier.

Divorce is a grown-up problem. People get divorced for many different reasons and all the reasons have to do with grown-ups and grown-up problems.

Sometimes parents get married too young, sometimes grown-ups hurt each other too much, sometimes they just grow apart, sometimes they just argue too much, sometimes money makes them fall out, sometimes they meet other people and fall in love with them. There are lots and lots of reasons that have **NOTHING** to do with you.

REMEMBER, whatever is happening with your parents, they will **ALWAYS** love you.

YOU ARE NOT TO BLAME for your parents splitting up.

Writing in your Journal is not like homework, no one's going to mark it or judge you! In fact, no one has to see it unless you want to share it with someone.

You can't mess up your Journal or fill it in wrong – it's there to help you notice patterns, or ups and downs, in your feelings and to notice how you're dealing with the divorce as you're going through it.

No one is happy all the time. Good mental health is when you can be happy, sad, angry, frustrated or just plain fed up, while still knowing that you have bounce-back-ability, otherwise known as resilience.

Sometimes big or confusing feelings or questions might come up when you work through your Journal and it is a good idea to chat these through with someone. You can chat to your parents, teacher, aunt, uncle, grandparent or anyone that you trust, as it might help you feel better to share some of your mixed emotions.

YOUR NEW BEST FRIEND...

You have a **new best friend** – your Journal! It will help you come through this time HAPPIER, HEALTHIER and STRONGER.

YOUR JOURNAL IS A PLACE TO...

- **Explore** your feelings
- **Express** your worries, fears and anxieties
- **Release** how you are feeling about your parents' divorce in a safe place
- **Express** your anger, as there's probably a lot to vent about!
- Get your feelings out of your head, and out of your body, so you can **understand** them, and feel better
- **Learn** more about yourself and celebrate what makes you special, loveable and wonderful

A photo of me...

...that I love!

ALL ABOUT ME

My **name** is: ....

I am .... years old

My **hair** colour: ....

My **eye** colour: ....

What I'm **good** at: ....

....

....

....

What I like doing for **fun**: ....

....

....

....

My favourite **colour** is: ....

My favourite **TV programme** is: ....

....

My favourite **film** is: ....

....

My favourite **game** to play is: ....

....

My favourite **sport** is:......................................

....

My **hobbies** are:...

....

....

....

My **best friend** is:..

My favourite way to **relax** is:..............................

....

....

My favourite **food** is:.......................................

....

My favourite **subject** at school is:........................

....

My favourite **animal** is:.....................................

....

My favourite **music** is:......................................

....

My favourite **place** is:......................................

....

My favourite **present** ever was:...........................

....

Things that make me **happy**: ....

....

....

....

....

....

ABOUT MY FAMILY

My parents' names are: ....

I live with my: ....

I have ....brothers and sisters.

I am the .... child in my family.

I am in.................... year at school.

I live in: ....

HERE'S A PICTURE OF MY WHOLE FAMILY
(why not include your grandparents, cousins, uncles and aunts?).

GETTING MARRIED

People have been getting married for thousands of years. They've also been separating for thousands of years too, because living together isn't always easy.

Why do you think people get married or live together? ....

....

....

What are some of the great things about living together? ....

....

....

What are some of the difficult things about living together? ....

....

....

Why do parents have kids? ....

....

....

FAMILIES COME IN ALL SHAPES AND SIZES. DRAW SOME DIFFERENT TYPES OF FAMILIES.

WHAT IS A SEPARATION?

A separation is when two people who are married decide to live apart and are deciding what to do next about their marriage. Sometimes a separation is a difficult thing to understand and to talk about and sometimes you can feel caught in the middle. Has this happened to you?

Lots of children want their parents to stay together, but sometimes things have got so bad that some children feel relieved when their parents decide to separate.

Sometimes it's better for a family when parents separate.

A separation can be for a short or a long time. It just depends.

How do you feel? ....

....

....

....

DRAW WHAT SEPARATION LOOKS LIKE TO YOU.

WHAT DOES DIVORCE MEAN?

A divorce is when two people decide that they don't want to be married. They feel that they can't live happily together any more. They decide that they don't want to be married but they will always be your parents, no matter what.

DRAW A PICTURE OF YOUR HOME AND FAMILY BEFORE THE DIVORCE IN THE BOX BELOW.

HOW DID IT FEEL TO DRAW THAT PICTURE? COLOUR THE SHAPES BELOW THAT EXPRESS HOW YOU FEEL.

If some of your feelings aren't shown, write in your own ones in the empty shapes.

Safe

Secure

Loved

Angry

Scared

Guilty

Worried

HOW DO YOU FEEL TODAY?

DRAW, DOODLE, SCRIBBLE, COLOUR OR WRITE ABOUT ANYTHING YOU WANT ON THIS PAGE!

WE ALL CHANGE!

DRAW A PICTURE OF YOURSELF HERE.

DRAW OR FIND PHOTOS OF YOURSELF GROWING UP AT DIFFERENT AGES.

As a baby

As a toddler

Starting nursery

Going to school

Last year

Last week

YOU'VE CHANGED! Just like you,
grown-ups change too.

SPECIAL MEMORIES

CHOOSE 4 MEMORIES THAT ARE SPECIAL TO YOU
AND DRAW THEM OR FIND PHOTOS THAT YOU CAN
STICK IN HERE.

SELF-ESTEEM

1. **I am special** because...

   Draw or write all the things that you are good at, proud of
   yourself for, or have achieved from the things that you enjoy (like
   dancing, football, Lego®, Minecraft® or spelling, drawing, etc.!).

2. What people **love**, **respect** and **admire** about me...

   Go and ask your friends and family and write or draw what they say!

3. What is **important** to me and makes me **happy**...

Things like my cat, bike, bedroom, tablet, toys, spending time with Grandma, watching films with family on Friday nights and going out with friends.

4. Ways to **support** me at home and at school...

Write down things that your family, teacher and school could do to help you.

5. What's working and not working for me.

Write down what is and isn't helping you right now.

What's working?

. . . .

. . . .

. . . .

. . . .

. . . .

. . . .

What's not working?

. . . .

. . . .

. . . .

. . . .

. . . .

. . . .

THINGS THAT STAY THE SAME

When your parents get divorced there are lots of things that change and that can feel scary. But it can help to remember that lots of things stay the same too. You can help yourself feel calmer and safe by reminding yourself regularly of all the things that stay the same.

Write down or draw all the things that stay the same. Things like being able to watch your favourite TV show, going to the same school, having the same friends, having your brother and sister with you, the love of your grandparents, your favourite food, your birthday, the colour of your eyes, going to ballet, football training and things that you do for fun.

Make a copy of all the things that have stayed the same and put it up in your bedroom or in a special place, so when you feel scared or upset, you can go and have a look at your list and it will make you feel better.

FEELING SAD

When people feel sad they show it in different ways. For example, some children will cry when they are sad. Some won't. Some might want to spend time with others. Some would prefer to be on their own for a while.

It's normal to feel sad now and again and lots of things can make you feel sad. Sometimes they're big things, sometimes they're small.

Life is full of ups and downs. We all go through times when things are going well and other times that are more stressful.

You may feel sad, upset or worried about having a row with your friend, disagreeing with your brothers and sisters over something that's not fair, starting a new school, not being invited to a party, moving house, a disappointment, not getting your own way or your parents separating.

DRAW HERE HOW YOU SHOW THAT YOU ARE FEELING SAD.

There are no silly reasons for feeling sad. Sadness, like all emotions, has a job to do as it tells you that something needs your attention.

The temptation can be to push your sadness away or to pretend that it doesn't exist, or to cover it up with another emotion like anger. But sadness will pass. Be **patient, kind** and **gentle** to yourself and **talk to someone** about your feelings as that will help you feel better.

Being able to understand your emotions and how to deal with them is a kind of SUPERPOWER.

HOW TO HELP YOURSELF WHEN YOU FEEL SAD AND UPSET

Here are some ways that you can help yourself to feel better when you're feeling sad and upset. **Circle** some of the things you will remember to do next time you feel sad.

- Stroke your cat

- Go and play in the garden with your dog

- Read a funny book

- Listen to your favourite music

- Chat to family

- Text or video call your friend

- Tell someone

- Put on your pyjamas and watch a funny video

- Go swimming

- Kick a ball around in the garden

- Ride your bike

- Ask for a hug

- Play a game

- Sing a song

ADD YOUR OWN WAYS OF FEELING BETTER:

- ....
- ....
- ....
- ....
- ....

- ....
- ....
- ....
- ....
- ....

HOW TO HELP YOURSELF WHEN YOU FEEL ANGRY

It's perfectly normal to feel angry about your parents' divorce but it's what you **CHOOSE** to do with your anger that's important.

When people feel angry they show it in many different ways. Some are safe and healthy, but some are not.

HEALTHY

- Go outside and stomp your feet
- Go outside and shout very loudly
- Go outside and run about
- Go outside and kick a ball
- Take some deep breaths
- Have a cry

UNHEALTHY

- Hit someone
- Bite someone
- Scratch someone
- Throw sticks at someone
- Say mean, hurtful or unkind things to someone
- Break things

WHAT IS A SAFE WAY TO LET OUT YOUR ANGER? DRAW IT BELOW.

PUNCH ME!

WHAT ARE YOUR TRIGGERS TO FEELING ANGRY? WHAT IS IT THAT STARTS YOU OFF FEELING ANGRY?

....

....

....

When I'm angry, I can calm myself by:

- Deep breathing
- Punching a pillow
- Taking a break
- Talking about it

FEELING HELPLESS

You might feel helpless when you can't do your homework, finish a jigsaw or cross a busy road by yourself until you ask for help, but divorce is different. Children often feel helpless when their parents divorce because there is nothing they can do to change the situation. That's because divorce is a decision made by your parents. They will be making lots of decisions that you won't have any control over and that might make you feel helpless.

You can't make them get back together, get along better, or stop the divorce.

But there are safe ways to help yourself cope when you're feeling helpless.

Share your feelings with someone, tell your family how you're feeling, tell your teacher, or tell another grown-up you trust.

It also helps to think of all the other ways in your life that you're **not** helpless as it helps to balance out your thoughts.

WRITE DOWN ALL THE THINGS YOU CAN DO WITHOUT ANYONE'S HELP, FROM TYING YOUR SHOELACES TO MAKING YOUR BED. WRITE DOWN WAYS THAT YOU ARE NOT HELPLESS.

1. ....

2. ....

3. ....

4. ....

5. ....

6. ....

7. ....

8. ....

GET MOVING

Getting active helps you to release something called endorphins which are "feel good" hormones. So think about things you like to do to get your body moving – swimming, dancing, playing football, going to karate, running, jumping or stretching – as getting active will really help you to cope with stress, anxiety and change.

Sitting still or playing lots of games on your tablet or computer for hours can add to your stress – it makes you jittery, hyper and short-tempered, so take a break and **GET MOVING!**

DRAW SOME FUN THINGS YOU LIKE TO DO TO GET ACTIVE.

MINDFUL BREATHING

Meditating or being mindful and breathing deeply and slowly helps you to cope with stress.

Before you begin this mindfulness exercise make sure that you've turned off any distractions, such as the television or your video games, and be sure your mobile phone is on silent!

Go and find your favourite soft toy and then lie down on your back with your cuddly friend on your tummy. Focus all your attention on the rise and fall of your fluffy friend as you breathe in and out.

Say the words "in" and "out" as your soft toy goes up and down with your breath.

Do this slowly and deeply 5 times. You could do it for even more times if you enjoy doing it.

Notice how relaxed your body and mind are just from slowly breathing in and out.

Do this anytime you feel overwhelmed, frightened or anxious.

It helps to CALM your mind and body down.

HOW DO YOU FEEL TODAY?

DRAW, DOODLE, SCRIBBLE, COLOUR OR WRITE ABOUT ANYTHING YOU WANT ON THIS PAGE!

AFTER THE DIVORCE

DRAW A PICTURE OF YOUR HOME (OR HOMES) AND FAMILY AFTER THE DIVORCE IN THE BOX BELOW.

What are some of the things that are different about your family after the divorce?

....

....

....

What changes make you sad? ....

....

What changes make you angry? ....

....

What changes make you fed up? ....

....

What changes do you like? ....

....

What would you like to say to your parents that
they haven't heard from you yet?

....

....

....

How would that make you feel? ....

....

Pick a good time (not when you're doing your
homework or meant to be asleep!) to tell your parent
how you feel so they can listen properly to you.

When would that be? (Be specific – e.g. after football
training; on Wednesday evening after dinner.)

....

How would that make you feel? ....

....

DRAW A HOUSE BELOW. ON, BESIDE OR UNDER THE HOUSE, WRITE A LIST OF 5 THINGS YOU'D LIKE TO STAY THE SAME DURING THE DIVORCE. SHARE YOUR PICTURE WITH YOUR PARENT.

DIFFERENT HOUSES – DIFFERENT RULES

When your parents live in different places, they will sometimes make up different rules than when you were all living together. Some of the rules may be the same, and some of the rules will be different. That might be a bit confusing at first but it's a bit like remembering that there are rules for walking around a swimming pool and different rules for walking around a museum. You'll get the hang of them!

Make a note of the different rules below.

RULES WHEN I'M AT ....'S HOUSE

- ....
- ....

- ....
- ....
- ....
- ....

RULES WHEN I'M AT ....'S HOUSE

- ....
- ....
- ....
- ....
- ....
- ....

Have a chat about the rules with your parents.
Perhaps you could make some suggestions.

WHAT'S IMPORTANT TO YOU

On this page write down, draw or find photos of all the things that are important to you (your games, your tablet, your shell collection, a soft toy, your football trophies, your orange karate belt, your dog, cat or gerbil, your brother and sister, your best friend or your Grandad). You can even write down things like jumping into your parent's bed on a Saturday morning, eating toast and strawberry jam, watching cartoons or going on holiday!

SHARING TIME

One of the big changes during a divorce is that you'll probably have to share and split your time between two houses. Lots of kids find this really hard at first.

This time can be hard as it reminds you that your parents are divorced. It can be difficult or stressful as they might argue. It might be hard because you might forget some things. It might be hard as you feel sad and miss the parent you are leaving.

There are 2 steps to making this time easier.

Step 1: **RECOGNISE** and **ACCEPT** your sadness.

Step 2: **DO SOMETHING** to take your mind off it.

Lots of children take a photo of their other parent, or bring a special toy or game, or a special birthday present, or a special note with them to their other parent's home.

Lots of children have their mobile phones with them so that they can text or call their other parent for a chat.

Lots of children need a special big hug before they leave.

Lots of children have a little cry to let their feelings out.

THINGS TO TAKE YOUR MIND OFF THE JOURNEY

- Bring your favourite book in the car with you
- Play 'I spy' in the car
- Play the 'License Plate' Game where you make up words with the last 3 letters of the car in front of you
- Count the post boxes

What other ideas have you thought of?

. . . .

. . . .

. . . .

. . . .

WHAT TO DO WHEN PARENTS ARGUE

It's perfectly normal for you to feel upset, scared or fed up when your parents argue. Here is a simple thing to do to help yourself. Remember to **TAG**!

T - **TELL** them how you feel

A - **ASK** them to stop, but if they don't...

G - **GO** somewhere safe (like your bedroom), away from them so you don't have to listen.

THINGS TO SAY

I feel hurt/angry/upset when you put me in the middle of a row.

I feel guilty when you ask me to tell you what happens at my other parent's house.

I feel sad when you criticise each other. Please don't make me take sides. I love you both.

NOT ALL BAD

When parents get divorced they sometimes want to blame each other, but no parent is all bad or all good either. It's important to remember that when people are hurt, they sometimes say things that they don't mean later.

Think of a time when you fell out with a friend. Now think of a time when you made up. Sometimes it takes grown-ups time to heal from the stress, anger and sadness of divorce too.

Sometimes parents don't smile very much, they might lose weight, put on weight, get angry over little things, say mean things to you, cry a lot, or drink too much, as they find divorce stressful, but remember your parents' divorce is **NOT YOUR FAULT** and they love you very much. If you are worried about one of your parents **TELL SOMEONE** like your teacher, Aunt, Uncle, Grandma, doctor, school nurse or another grown-up you trust so they can help.

MY FEELINGS

I used to think we were ....

but now I think ....

....

I wonder if ....

....

I also think about ....

....

When I think about my family not being together any more, it makes me feel

....

....

I worry about ....

....

I also worry about ....

....

I try not to think about ....

....

I also try not to think about ....

....

What I like about my family is ....

....

When you feel UPSET or ANGRY with both your parents or one of your parents, it helps to REMEMBER all the THINGS YOU LOVE about them.

WHAT I LOVE ABOUT MY ....
(name of parent)

....

....

I love it when they ....

....

I love doing these things with them: ....

....

We laugh when ....

....

My favourite thing for us to do together is ....

....

What I don't like is when ....

....

because it makes me feel ....

....

I wish they knew that ....

....

WHAT I LOVE ABOUT MY ....
(name of other parent)

....

....

I love it when they ....

....

I love doing these things with them: ....

....

We laugh when ....

....

My favourite thing for us to do together is ....

....

What I don't like is when ....

....

because it makes me feel ....

....

I wish they knew that ....

....

THINGS YOU LIKE DOING

DURING THE SUMMER HOLIDAYS, CHLOE ENJOYS GOING FISHING WITH HER DAD. WRITE DOWN 6 THINGS YOU LIKE DOING WITH ONE OF YOUR PARENTS.

1. ....

....

2. ....

....

3. ....

....

4. ....

....

5. ....

....

6. ....

....

DURING THE SUMMER HOLIDAYS, JOE ENJOYS GOING SWIMMING WITH HIS MUM. WRITE DOWN 6 THINGS YOU LIKE DOING WITH YOUR OTHER PARENT.

1. ....

....

2. ....

....

3. ....

....

4. ....

....

5. ....

....

6. ....

....

QUESTIONS ABOUT DIVORCE

Divorce can be upsetting and frightening because it is full of changes, but people describe how they feel about it in different ways.

WHAT WORDS WOULD YOU USE TO DESCRIBE YOUR PARENTS' DIVORCE?

Write down your thoughts in the clouds below.

Some children have a lot of questions about their parents' divorce. What questions do you have? Things like: "Where am I going to live?" "Will I have to change school?" "Will I still see Grandma and Grandad on Wednesdays after school?" "How often will I see the parent I don't live with?"

Write down your questions below. Then find a good time to ask your parents about them.

....

....

....

....

....

....

....

....

....

....

SOMEONE TO TALK TO

When Tom wants to talk to someone about his feelings, he talks to his sister. Sometimes he talks to his Auntie Rosie, his Grandma or his teacher at school.

WRITE DOWN THE NAMES OF THE PEOPLE YOU CAN YOU TALK TO ABOUT YOUR FEELINGS.

When I'm upset, I can talk to...

- ....
- ....
- ....
- ....
- ....

BIG FEELINGS

When families go through divorces, kids feel a lot of things they often don't know how to express. Sometimes your parents are so busy coping with what's happening that they seem a bit preoccupied and busy and don't seem to have as much time for you as they used to, or are not as good at listening to you as they were before.

This is all perfectly normal and doesn't mean they don't love you – it's just they have a lot on their mind and have a lot of grown-up stuff to sort out.

Some kids feel guilty about their parents breaking up and say things like, "If I had stayed in my bed at night instead of jumping into my parents' bed they'd probably still be together" or "If I had done better at school – they'd probably still be together."

None of this is true.

It's not easy being married and it's not easy divorcing – but it's **never** your fault. Adults make mistakes, meet other people, fall out of friendship and fall out of love and some kids feel guilty that their parents are getting divorced, but it's between your parents and it's nothing that you've done.

Some kids feel scared and don't know what to expect, and some kids feel angry at their parents for deciding to divorce as it changes everything. Sometimes kids feel all of these emotions at the same time!

Sometimes it can be hard to deal with the **big feelings** we have. They can feel overwhelming – sometimes bigger than we think we can handle.

USE THE SPACE BELOW TO WRITE OR DRAW YOUR BIG FEELINGS. IT MIGHT HELP TO GET HOW YOU FEEL DOWN ON THE PAGE.

SINCE THE FAMILY SEPARATED

Since the family separated I miss.............................

....

....

....

I wonder if we will ever...................................

....

....

When I'm alone I think about...........................

....

....

Sometimes I could use some help with ....

....

....

It's OK to feel disappointed or angry. We can't always control our feelings but we can control how we REACT and RESPOND to them.

Sometimes when we feel angry, disappointed, upset or frightened we say or do things we shouldn't.

We need to figure out healthy ways to handle our strong feelings in a better, more positive way.

In the shapes below, write down some of the ways you sometimes react when you're upset. Then next to each shape, colour in the smiley face if it is a good, healthy way to react or the frowning face if it's not a healthy way to react.

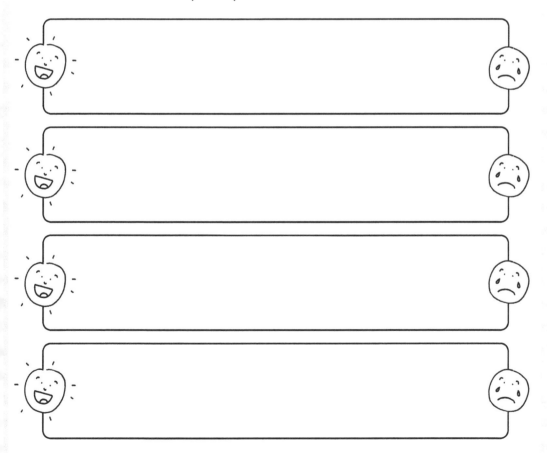

WRITING LETTERS

During a hard time, like a divorce, there are lots of things you wish you could say that perhaps you feel you can't really say in case it upsets your parent.

One great way to feel better is to write letters that you never send!

You can write letters to your Mum, Dad, Grandma, best friend...anyone you like!

So just imagine that you could write a letter to one of your parents. What would you like to tell them, what would you like them to know, what things would you change or do differently than what's happening at the moment?

Don't hold back – go for it!

Dear ....

....

....

....

....

....

....

....

....

....

....

....

From ....

HIGH FIVE!

On each finger, write or draw something that will keep you **HAPPY**, **HEALTHY** and feeling **POSITIVE**.

Remember to SMILE

S SPEND TIME with your friends

M MOVE about and get physical as it releases feel good hormones – dance, sing, jump or run

I GET INVOLVED and interested in a hobby, learn karate, play the guitar, join a chess club

L LAUGH, smile and be silly – it's OK to still have fun and chill out

E ENGAGE and ENJOY your life – yes things have changed but go out, have fun, hang out with your friends, play with your pets and have fun with your family

REMEMBER YOU ARE GREAT!

5 THINGS THAT I LIKE ABOUT MYSELF:

1. ....

....

2. ....

....

3. ....

....

4. ....

....

5. ....

....

HOW DO YOU FEEL TODAY?

DRAW, DOODLE, SCRIBBLE, COLOUR OR WRITE ABOUT ANYTHING YOU WANT ON THIS PAGE!

PARENTS DIVORCE, BUT FAMILY IS FOREVER

I always say that "divorce is a process, not an event". That means that it takes time to get used to it.

REMEMBER, JUST BECAUSE THINGS CHANGE, IT DOESN'T MEAN THEY END.

PARENTS DIVORCE, BUT FAMILY IS FOREVER

You may see your parents on different days but they're still your parents and they love you. So make the most of your time together. Hang out, read together, watch your favourite TV show together, eat together, play in the park together, cuddle up, talk, chat, share and laugh.

LIVING IN TWO HOMES

Living in two homes is very DIFFERENT from living in one. It takes time to get used to it. You may feel unsettled for a while until it feels normal. You probably need to get more ORGANISED and have two sets of things to make your life easier.

IN THE CHART BELOW WRITE DOWN A LIST OF THINGS THAT YOU COULD KEEP AT EACH HOME TO MAKE THINGS EASIER.

Things like pyjamas, toothbrushes, school shoes, school shirts, PE kit, coats.

At home with my .... (name of parent) I can keep	At home with my .... (name of other parent) I can keep

SO HOW'S IT GOING?

THINK ABOUT ONE OF YOUR PARENTS.

What's it like when you're at their house?

....

....

What do you enjoy about being with them?

....

....

What would make it more enjoyable?

....

....

How would you like it to be?

....

....

What special things do you do together that
you love?

....

....

....

NOW THINK ABOUT YOUR OTHER PARENT.

What's it like when you're at their house?

....

....

What do you enjoy about being with them?

....

....

What would make it more enjoyable?

....

....

How would you like it to be?

....

....

What special things do you do together that you love?

....

....

....

MY FAMILY TREE

Even if your family lives in two different places, you are still a family.

CELEBRATE ALL THE PEOPLE IN YOUR FAMILY BY DRAWING A FAMILY TREE.

What are your favourite things about your brother?

. . . .

. . . .

What are your favourite things about your sister?

. . . .

. . . .

What are your favourite things about your Grandma?

. . . .

. . . .

What are your favourite things about your Grandad?

. . . .

. . . .

What are your favourite things about your aunts?

. . . .

. . . .

What are your favourite things about your uncles?

....

....

What are your favourite things about your cousins?

....

....

DRAW SOME FUNNY MEMORIES OF BEING WITH YOUR FAMILY IN THE BOX.

NEW TRADITIONS

You can start new traditions in your family.

Some families get a real Christmas tree for Christmas when they didn't before; some families go bike riding every Sunday; some eat at the table every evening to chat and catch up on everyone's day.

What new traditions would you like to start and with which parent? Try to think of some new traditions you can have for each of your houses.

New tradition	With...

HOW I'M DOING

It helps to see how you're doing and how far you've come in handling the changes so you can pat yourself on the back, celebrate and do a happy dance (if you want to!) about how you've coped through a really hard time.

REMEMBER, YOU ARE AMAZING!

We all cope well at times and wobble and lose the plot at other times. So don't beat yourself up if you have found it difficult. Just imagine you are up in a spaceship looking down at yourself and you can see really clearly the bigger picture of how far you've come.

SO LET'S TAKE STOCK.

Before the divorce I felt ....

....

When my parents told me that they were divorcing I felt

....

....

When my parents moved to different places I felt

. . . .

. . . .

If one or both of your parents have met someone else, how did that make you feel?

. . . .

. . . .

How I feel about my Mum now: . . . .

. . . .

How I feel about my Dad now: . . . .

. . . .

How I feel about myself now: . . . .

. . . .

What I've learnt about myself: . . . .

. . . .

Today I feel . . . .

. . . .

MY IDEAS

Kids have lots of great ideas for their parents about divorce. Here is a selection of great things that kids have said.

- STOP SHOUTING!
- Tell me what's going on!
- Don't put me in the middle and ask me questions about Dad
- Keep to the rules – you agreed to them!
- Don't tell me bad things about Mummy
- Try to be nice to one another
- Don't keep buying me toys. It doesn't make me feel better
- Don't make me like your new girlfriend/ boyfriend
- Stop fighting about money

WHAT WOULD YOU LIKE YOUR PARENTS TO KNOW?

- ....
- ....
- ....
- ....
- ....

THE LEGAL STUFF

Going through a divorce is painful and stressful for everyone including your parents. Sometimes they can sort things out themselves, sometimes they need help from a mediating lawyer to help them, sometimes they argue so much they need a Judge in a Court Room to sort it out for them.

It can be quite complicated but lawyers are people who help both your parents understand the laws about what's fair in a divorce.

If they need a Judge to help them sort it all out, the Judge will decide when you see your Dad or Mum, how often, and they will help your parents decide who you'll live with, or how you'll share your time with both of them. They help sort out the money side of things too, and how to share it out fairly.

Legal stuff can be pretty confusing. Here are some new words and what they mean.

- **CUSTODY** is the decision about who is responsible for you until you are 18. This can include where you will live and where you go to school. Lots of parents work together to make you happy and settled and because they love you. The person who has custody has the final say.

- **SHARED OR JOINT CARE** is when both of your parents agree to bring you up together by sharing all the decisions but they will be living separately and apart.

- **CHILD SUPPORT OR MAINTENANCE** is the money that one parent gives another to help pay for all the things you need from school shoes to holidays. The lawyers or Judges help your parents sort out what is fair. Parents do argue quite a lot over this bit sometimes.

- **CONTACT ARRANGEMENTS** are the rules about when, where and how often you will see or stay with each of your parents. There are lots of different types of arrangements.

WRITE DOWN HOW OFTEN YOU'D LIKE TO SEE YOUR DAD AND MUM AND WHAT SORT OF ARRANGEMENTS YOU'D PREFER AND THEN CHAT THEM THROUGH WITH YOUR PARENTS.

. . . .

. . . .

. . . .

. . . .

. . . .

. . . .

89

STAY CLOSE

After Priyansh and Ananya's parents divorced their Dad moved to another town. To keep close to their Dad, Priyansh and Ananya video call, email or WhatsApp their Dad every other day with their news.

WHAT WOULD YOU LIKE TO DO TO STAY CLOSE TO YOUR MUM OR DAD WHEN YOU AREN'T WITH THEM? WRITE DOWN 2 THINGS YOU CAN DO TO STAY CLOSE AND HOW OFTEN YOU'D LIKE TO CHAT.

1. ....

....

....

2. ....

....

....

How often I'd like to chat: ....

....

....

WAYS TO RELAX

Going through a divorce is stressful so
Maria loves to play with her brother
Ben. It relaxes her and they both have fun.

WRITE DOWN 4 THINGS YOU LIKE TO DO WITH YOUR FAMILY TO RELAX AND HAVE FUN.

1. ....

2. ....

3. ....

4. ....

WRITE DOWN 4 THINGS YOU LIKE TO DO BY YOURSELF TO RELAX.

1. ....

2. ....

3. ....

4. ....

WRITE DOWN 4 THINGS YOU LIKE TO DO WITH YOUR FRIENDS TO RELAX AND HAVE FUN.

1. ....

2. ....

3. ....

4. ....

QUIET TIME

When Chris wants some quiet time she goes to read in the garden.

WRITE DOWN 4 PLACES YOU CAN GO TO CHILL OUT.

1. I could go to ....

   and ....

2. I could go to ....

   and ....

3. I could go to ....

   and ....

4. I could go to ....

   and ....

OTHER KIDS

It can feel like you're the only one going through a tough time so it helps to remember that lots of other children are going through exactly what you are too.

Can you think of any kids at school, or that you know, whose parents have split up? Can you think of any kids in books, films or TV shows that have gone through a divorce?

Write down who they are and how they handled the divorce below.

Who?	How did they handle it?

Talking to other children or adults can help you feel that you're not alone so if you feel comfortable have a chat with them. A problem shared is a problem halved.

Pick one of the people or characters that you wrote about and imagine that you could ask them to give you some good advice – what would you ask and what might they say to you? Write it down here.

. . . .

. . . .

. . . .

NO MATTER WHAT

Your parents may have stopped loving each other but that doesn't mean that they've stopped loving you. The love in a marriage is different to the love your parents feel for you. You are ALWAYS going to be loved and be SPECIAL to them.

WRITE OR DRAW THE REASONS WHY YOUR PARENTS LOVE YOU – THINK OF WHAT THEY ADMIRE ABOUT YOU, ARE PROUD OF YOU FOR, AND ENJOY ABOUT YOU. GO AND ASK THEM TOO!

SUPPORTING EACH OTHER

Your whole family needs you to show them that you care for and love them too – so how can you show your parents and brothers and sisters that you love and care for them?

WRITE SOME IDEAS DOWN IN THE HEARTS.

THE MAGIC WAND EXERCISE

I want you to relax and to find a quiet space to just float off into a lovely daydream.

Relax your body, let your arms and legs feel really heavy, and take really deep, slow breaths and just enjoy the feelings of relaxing.

Just float out and imagine that you can see yourself 3 years from now.

What do you think your life will be like?

What are you doing?

What can you see?

What can you hear?

How do you look?

How do you feel?

What's lovely about your life now?

Just relax and keep breathing deeply and slowly and enjoy seeing your life calmer and settled and happy...

DRAW A PICTURE OF YOURSELF THERE IN 3 YEARS' TIME.

THE TOOTHBRUSH TECHNIQUE

Every morning when you are brushing your teeth I want to you look at yourself in the mirror deep into your own eyes and say out loud one thing that makes you **SPECIAL**. Things like...

- I'm friendly
- I'm thoughtful
- I'm funny
- I'm kind
- I'm good at football/dancing/cricket/running
- I'm respectful
- I'm honest
- I'm good at maths
- I'm good at ICT
- I try new things

PRACTISE doing this exercise every morning for at least 2 weeks and it'll become a new fantastic habit and you'll start to feel amazing. It's not showing off, as you're just remembering why you are truly amazing.

Then every evening say out loud, when you are brushing your teeth, one thing you are **GRATEFUL** for. Things like...

- I have a lovely warm home
- I have a great brother or sister
- I go to a great school
- I have great friends
- I have running water
- I have lovely food to eat
- I have a lovely Granny
- I love my dog, Freddie
- I have loads of great toys
- I have a great Mum

Getting into an Attitude of Gratitude is a wonderful way to stay positive and, with practice, every night when you brush your teeth you'll create a wonderful new way of thinking and feeling.

Go on, try it!

THE CIRCLE OF CONFIDENCE

Here is a little fun thing to try.

Jump up (after you've read through what to do!) and do this fun exercise that will make you feel fantastic.

Imagine all the times when you *have* felt confident. Just relax and remember all the things you're good at, and love doing and feel fantastic when you're doing them.

Now imagine you are drawing a circle on the floor in front of you.

Make it shiny, or sparkly, or your favourite colour.

Pick one of those times when you felt really positive and confident and step into the circle thinking about it.

Remember it as if you were really there, notice what you can see (the people, the objects, the colours), remember what you hear (the sounds, the happy voice inside your own head, the happy voices of other people, or perhaps the peaceful silence), and remember exactly what you feel (positive, confident, relaxed). Now turn up the experience by brightening the colours, making the sounds much louder and the positive, confident feelings really strong.

Now step out of the circle when you're ready, and bring all those happy, positive thoughts and feelings back with you and squeeze your hand into a fist so you put all that confidence into your own hands. Take a look around the room and then repeat everything again three more times.

You have now created a **MAGIC CIRCLE** so that wherever you are, you can imagine the circle, step into it and recreate that confident feeling. Fab, eh?

TIME TO WRITE A STORY

WHAT IS YOUR STORY ABOUT THE DIVORCE OF YOUR PARENTS?

Write a story as if you are telling a new friend you've just met about what happened, or you could make up a story about someone else going through a divorce.

You could write about things like:

- What happened to you?
- How did you feel?
- What did you do?
- What was the most difficult for you?
- How did your parents support you?
- What did not work for you?

....

....

....

....

....

....

....

....

....

....

Now draw some pictures to illustrate it.

HISTORY TIMELINE

Lots of children worry about the future. They worry about what is going to happen to them and if their lives will ever be normal again. So you're not alone if you worry. Creating a timeline can help you to put the current events of what you are going through into perspective.

It can help you to see that you have experienced many good things in the past, and that you have many years ahead of you to have fun and happy times with your family.

Perhaps you'd like to chat about your thoughts with one of your parents.

- Draw a long horizontal line on a sheet of paper.
- Label your birth at one end with a star.
- Label the present time somewhere in the middle.
- Mark significant events that have occurred in your life between the "birth" star and the "present" mark. Perhaps you could mark in the birth of your brother or sister, getting your family pet, starting school, moving house, learning to read, learning to ride a bike, going through divorce, joining your team or club, the death of one of your relatives and wonderful holidays.

- Now extend the line and make it longer and mark in events that you hope will happen in the future. Have fun with this part – relax and enjoy thinking of lovely things you'd like to do in the future.

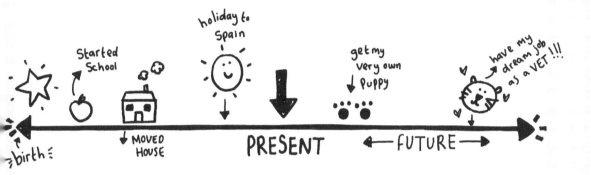

TIME CAPSULE

Making a time capsule is a great way to feel better. There are many different kinds of containers that make good time capsules – large glass jars with tight lids, large manila envelopes, shoe boxes or drawstring bags. Have fun choosing, making, designing and creating.

Put all your worries into your time capsule. Put in drawings, photographs, special treasures, stories, anything that you feel like including.

Here are some ideas:

TIME CAPSULE QUESTIONS

- Who are your friends?
- Who is part of your family now?
- Who will be part of your family in the future?
- Where will you be living in 1 year? Five years?
- What kinds of things do you like to do?
- What would you like to learn how to do in the future?
- What do you want to be when you grow up?

After you have made your time capsule make sure you seal it carefully.

Where are you going to store it?

I wonder when you'll want to open it – in 1 year, on a certain birthday, or 5 years from the divorce?

Whenever you decide to open it, it will be fun to see what's happened to you since you made your time capsule.

YOU = AMAZING

You've come a long way. You should be proud of yourself.

By keeping your own Journal you have taken some really grown-up steps towards feeling **HEALTHY** and **HAPPIER**. You have become **STRONGER**. This doesn't mean you'll never have tough times again but now you'll know how to help yourself.

You may decide to share your Journal with your parents, or you may decide to keep some parts of your Journal private and to yourself and that's OK – it's a good thing. That's being respectful to yourself.

You're amazing – you've learnt so much about yourself and how to take care of yourself through a tough time.

CONGRATULATIONS!

WELL DONE!

Keep this Journal to help you remember what you've learnt. Take it out if you need a reminder that you're a great person.

How has this Journal helped you? Make a list of the 10 things you've learnt by keeping your Journal.

1. ....

2. ....

3. ....

4. ....

5. ....

6. ....

7. ....

8. ....

9. ....

10. ....

Well done on completing your Journal!

NOTES FOR ADULTS

SUGGESTIONS FOR PARENTS

It's very important to explain to your child that this is a different kind of book. This is a Journal where your child can share their feelings and thoughts or simply process what's happening to them for themselves. It won't be marked, they won't be judged and it is totally up to them how they use it.

Young children may need to have the Journal read aloud to them and to do the Journal little and often.

Some children prefer to write and draw in their Journal at their own pace and in their own time. They may enjoy picking and choosing the order in which they write in it. Let your child decide for themselves how they'd like to use their Journal. They will enjoy feeling in control of the process and exploring their thoughts.

Help your child to decide a safe place to keep their Journal.

Let your child know that they can write in their Journal whenever they like.

Make sure your child has plenty of writing and drawing materials available. It's also a good idea to buy new pens and pencils to make the Journal important and special. It helps to make the process of writing in their Journal important.

If you are reading the Journal with your child and doing it together, pick a quiet time, turn off the TV, and put away your mobile phone. Choose a private place, create a safe space and focus on really listening to your child without interrupting or making them feel judged or guilty about what may come up. This is about helping your child feel heard, understood and supported while they go through this life-changing event. Be accepting and non-judgemental. There are no right or wrong answers to their feelings and experiences. Accept everything and ponder and reflect later about what you discover.

Some children may want to read through the Journal without participating in the drawing and writing to start with. Use the opportunity to just listen and share the questions. Don't force them and don't rush them.

Sometimes the Journal can help you correct

misunderstandings or misinformation or confusion if your child has got the wrong end of the stick. Keep to the facts, park up your own emotions and remember to divorce with dignity. This is not a time to criticise their other parent.

When your child is tired or has had enough, respect their wishes. Divorce is a process, not an event, and children need time to process their emotions in their own time.

Parents, teachers, counsellors or therapists may find the Journal helpful in seeing the divorce from the child's perspective.

SUGGESTIONS FOR TEACHERS

Thousands of children experience the difficulties of divorce every year, and in spite of their parents' best intentions, divorce always has both long-term and short-term effects on children.

Some children due to their circumstances, personalities or sensitivity will be particularly vulnerable to the changes that divorce inevitably brings.

This Journal is an entirely new way to help children through a divorce. The activities in this Journal will teach children some new emotional and social skills, empowering them with ways of coping so they can become more resilient.

Children learn emotional intelligence skills just like

they learn academic or sporting skills – through practice, encouragement and patience.

Some aspects of this Journal can be done alone; some could be done in small groups. You could encourage some activities to be completed with your support and for some to be completed with the child's parents.

Some children whose parents are divorcing will experience depression, anxiety, anger or behavioural problems. Some children will cope better than others, but if you are at all concerned about a child then seek professional help for them.

There is no right or wrong way to use this Journal and it may take several years for a child to feel life is "normal" after experiencing a divorce. A positive, respectful, patient approach is all that's needed.

When a class has a number of children from a separated or divorced family, sharing a book with the whole group can help children begin to talk about their individual situations with their school peers, free from finger-pointing, judgement or criticism.

It's not a good idea to point out the children in the class from a separated or divorced family, but rather to allow them to speak up for themselves if they feel comfortable. It is reassuring to a child to know that they are not the only one going through this experience.

Children using the Journal in a classroom setting should never feel that it will be marked, judged or openly discussed unless they feel that they want to share their thoughts and feelings with others. It's not a school book.

This Journal will elicit strong emotions from some children, so create a safe space for a child to express themselves openly.

Using the Journal may help you to identify a child who is struggling and may need extra support and who would also benefit from being referred to a trained counsellor or therapist.

This Journal can be used individually, either by a teacher with the permission of the child's parents, or by recommending the Journal to a parent for use at home.

SUGGESTIONS FOR COUNSELLORS AND THERAPISTS

This Journal may be used in individual therapy to support the child in exploring their thoughts and emotions.

The act of writing in a journal can have a therapeutic effect on releasing strong emotions and can help children understand them. Writing can help a child organise, process and communicate their thoughts and emotions and reflect on them in a positive way.

Using a journal is a helpful activity for children who are reluctant to talk about what they are feeling or going through. For children who find it difficult to express their needs verbally or who have difficulty making decisions, keeping a journal of their thoughts is a good way to help them learn about themselves and gain clarity and confidence.

Journaling provides the opportunity for children to:

- Explore and identify emotions, helping them to build and develop emotional vocabulary
- Feel anger, express fear and communicate their thoughts and feelings
- Examine the pros and cons of something in order to be more decisive and confident
- Gain insight into their own and others' motives
- See the positives and the negatives
- Plan out difficult conversations ahead of time
- Consider new ideas and ways of managing big feelings

This Journal will also encourage cooperation, active participation and communication of thoughts and feelings.

You can work through the pages systematically or go through it in themes.

The Journal can be part of a holistic approach to helping children and can be used in conjunction with play therapy, art therapy, music, dance or drama.

OTHER RESOURCES

There are lots of great books for kids to read about divorce:

- All You Need Is Love: Celebrating Families of All Shapes and Sizes – Shanni Collins (ages 3–8)
- Always Mom, Forever Dad – Joanna Rowland and Penny Weber (ages 4–7)
- Candyfloss – Jacqueline Wilson (ages 9–14)
- The Case of the Scary Divorce – Carl Pickhardt (ages 9–12)
- Goggle Eyes – Anne Fine (ages 12–16)
- The Great Big Book of Families – Mary Hoffman and Ros Asquith (ages 4–8)
- Horse Dreams – Mary Vivian Johnson (ages 9–14)
- I Have a Question about Divorce: A Book for Children with Autism Spectrum Disorder or Other Special Needs – Arlen Grad Gaines and Meredith Englander Polsky (ages 5–11)
- It's Not the End of the World – Judy Blume (ages 8–13)
- The Suitcase Kid – Jacqueline Wilson (ages 9–11)
- You Make Your Parents Super Happy!: A Book about Parents Separating – Richy K. Chandler (ages 3–7)

You may also like to explore some books about anger, anxiety, sadness and other big feelings:

- Anger the Ancient Warrior: A Story and Workbook with CBT Activities to Master Your Anger – Sarah Trueman and Sara Godoli (ages 8-12)
- The Can-Do Kid's Journal: Discover Your Confidence Superpower! – Sue Atkins (ages 7-11)
- The Healthy Coping Colouring Book and Journal: Creative Activities to Help Manage Stress, Anxiety and Other Big Feelings – Pooky Knightsmith and Emily Hamilton (ages 8-14)
- Help! I've Got an Alarm Bell Going Off in My Head!: How Panic, Anxiety and Stress Affect Your Body – K. L. Aspden (ages 9-11)
- Outsmarting Worry: An Older Kid's Guide to Managing Anxiety – Dawn Huebner and Kara McHale (ages 9-13)
- Starving the Gremlin series (CBT workbooks on anger, anxiety, stress, exam stress, depression) – Kate Collins-Donnelly (separate books for ages 5-9 and 10+)

The organisations and resources listed below offer services directly to children and young people, or to the adults supporting them:

- **FAMILY LIVES**
  0800 800 2222
  The helpline provides information, advice, guidance and support on any aspect of parenting and family life. There is also online chat, an email support service and forums.

- **MY FAMILY'S CHANGING**
  These booklets are for children whose parents are separating. There are two versions, one for children under 12 and another for older children. They include stories from children who have been through similar experiences, games, and spaces for children to explore their feelings.

- **RESOLUTION**
  01689 820272
  The Resolution booklet 'Separation and Divorce - Helping parents to help children' is a practical guide to handling the emotional aspects of separation or divorce. It covers how children may react at different ages, tips for talking to children about separation, and managing your relationship with your child's other parent. Copies can be downloaded free from the website.

- **VOICES IN THE MIDDLE**
  www.voicesinthemiddle.com
  Voices in the Middle is a place where young people, aged 13 to 19 years old, whose parents are splitting up can find a place to share their voice and read helpful advice.

- **YOUNG MINDS**
  0808 802 5544
  Young Minds provides information and advice about mental health and emotional wellbeing for children, young people and their carers. The website provides help and information on how divorce and separation affect children, and parents and carers can call the helpline for free and confidential support.

ABOUT THE AUTHOR

Sue Atkins is an internationally recognised parenting expert, broadcaster, speaker and author of The Can-Do Kid's Journal: Discover Your Confidence Superpower!, Parenting Made Easy – How to Raise Happy Children, and Raising Happy Children for Dummies.

Sue offers practical guidance for bringing up happy, confident, well-behaved children, from toddlers to teens, and specialises in supporting families through divorce.

She regularly appears on the award-winning flagship ITV show This Morning and The Jeremy Vine Show on BBC Radio 2, and is the parenting expert for SKY News and for many BBC radio stations around the UK. She has a regular monthly parenting phone-in on BBC Radio Hereford & Worcester and her parenting articles are published all over the world.

For further details, please visit www.thesueatkins.com

by the same author

TV'S *THIS MORNING'S* PARENTING EXPERT

THE CAN-DO KID'S JOURNAL

DISCOVER YOUR CONFIDENCE SUPERPOWER!

SUE ATKINS

ILLUSTRATED BY AMY BRADLEY

THE CAN-DO KID'S JOURNAL
Discover Your Confidence Superpower!
Illustrated by Amy Bradley

ISBN 978 1 78775 271 9
eISBN 978 1 78775 272 6

Packed full of tried-and-tested activities and strategies that will empower children aged 7-11, this illustrated journal is perfect for developing resilience, confidence and a growth mindset. It offers kids a multitude of small changes they can make that will make a big difference in their day-to-day lives.

DOODLE YOUR WORRIES AWAY
A CBT Workbook for Children
Who Feel Worried or Anxious
Tanja Sharpe
ISBN 978 1 78775 790 5
eISBN 978 1 78775 791 2

**STARVING THE ANXIETY GREMLIN
FOR CHILDREN AGED 5-9**
A Cognitive Behavioural Therapy
Workbook on Anxiety Management
Kate Collins-Donnelly
ISBN 978 1 84905 492 8
eISBN 978 0 85700 902 9

ANGER THE ANCIENT WARRIOR
A Story and Workbook with CBT
Activities to Master Your Anger
Sarah Trueman and Sara Godoli
Illustrated by Dorian Cottereau
ISBN 978 1 78775 368 6
eISBN 978 1 78775 369 3

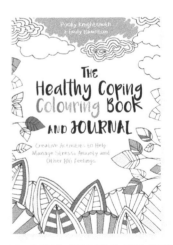

**THE HEALTHY COPING COLOURING
BOOK AND JOURNAL**
Creative Activities to Help Manage
Stress, Anxiety and Other Big Feelings
Pooky Knightsmith
Illustrated by Emily Hamilton
ISBN 978 1 78592 139 1
eISBN 978 1 78450 405 2